A Mother's

Love

Covers Sins

LINDA DIGGS

RELENTLESS
PUBLISHING

A Mother's Love Covers Sins
Copyright © 2020 by Linda Diggs.

Published by :
Relentless Publishing House
www.relentlesspublishing.com

RELENTLESS
PUBLISHING

ISBN: 978-1-948829-80-9

TABLE OF CONTENTS

1 Peter 4:8 NIV

Above all, love each other deeply, because love covers over a multitude of sins.

A Mother's Love

Introduction

My book God has given me is a journey where I moved by faith and trusted God all the way. I wasn't even supposed to write this book in my eyes, but God always has other plans concerning us. Jeremiah 29:11 says, *"For I know the thoughts that I think towards you, saith the Lord, thoughts of peace, and not of evil, to give you an expected end."* I have four non-published books that for some reason I can't find, so until then, God and I are going with this.

This is my story and I believe or let me say that our story should help others. Also that fact and truth that God spoke to me.

Me: *How can I help these women who are hurting and in so much pain when our story is different, when I haven't experienced what they have in the loss of their love one.*

God: *You have experienced Me!*

I thought it would go one way but even has I type I'm sure it has to go the way the Lord is leading me at this moment. This is a story of a mother's love and loss. I used both not because of me but many mothers are dealing with the love and loss of a love one but God has given me peace before the Lord called him home. My son, Monte that is!

Early Years

Is there something wrong? I inquired while he was laughing and Monte was smiling but quiet. Come to find out yes, he has one. I was upset and said some words to Monte. I have learned and seen with Monte no matter how much he tried to do the opposite of what God ordained for his life, he stuck out like a sore thumb, once said by one of his cousins. His doings were always pointed out and people always looked liked why he didn't even look like he should be doing that or be a part of that. He did exceptionally well in school and his teachers always talked well of him. We got through Elementary school and he graduated. On the other hand, we now enter middle school and teenage years. He went to Hamilton Middle and yes it all was new for the both of us. The time in a child's life when they have to make choices, who to hang with and who not to hang with. Well he was back and forth with his choices and got in trouble often whether suspension or cutting school. I chose to transfer him to Lombard Middle School in the center of a project environment even though we lived in another location. Not a great area but hoping for him, new faces and a new chance. Children always know more people than you think. I've heard of bad things concerning the school but I also hoped that what I taught him would follow him. Whether we teach our children correctly or not, this is the time in their life that they will deal with consequences of their choices. Well, he didn't always choose correctly and yes there were consequences. As his mother, I had to make some choices that he seemed to think weren't right, but for me I believed it was. There were times I wouldn't let him go to his paternal grandmother's house because I knew the lifestyle they lived. I've been around it myself and I didn't want him to go down that same spiral effect: hanging on corners, getting high, drunk or selling drugs. I had friends that would call me and say, "Isn't little Gary supposed to be over his Aunt's house?" They would see him hanging on corners doing Lord knows what. I would get in my car and go get him and bring him right home. He would get

□

suspended, not do homework and fail classes. What to do next? As a praying mother, I would go to God often for him. (1 Thessalonians 5:17) Going to God always gave me a next. (Isaiah 65:24) We went through a youth program that did homeschooling. God will give you a bridge in troubled waters. My fiancée would homeschool Monte until God moved again on his behalf.

November 23, 1987, he was born weighing 7lbs. 8 ounces. We named him Gary Lamonte Cooper, Jr. Even though I agreed with that name, I couldn't call him Gary with me being 19. That name seemed so old to me. Monte is what I loved and was comfortable calling him. Standing in the kitchen my water broke and me being new to having a baby, I thought I peed on myself lol. My Aunt had to inform me that my water broke and she put leg warmers on my legs. We were on our way to the hospital to welcome Monte. I was in labor 24 hours before he decided to join us outside of the womb. I can remember being told at the labor table that a different doctor was going to deliver him. A little scared and upset but I was more excited to see my little boy. As a young mother, I went on with their decision. He was born with a birthmark that looked like a map which covered one side of his stomach to the other side of his back. It was a greenish color. Of course, doctors wanted to inquire. Being a new mother, I was already in protective mode. I told them if it is not bothering him, then they were not bothering it. He lived his entire life with no complications of a rare mark.

Monte was a quiet little boy, very respectful and could be playful around other children. He was what we call a normal child. At the age of four years old a new sibling was coming. I found out I was pregnant and he would be a little jealous but I decided to include him in my whole process. I would let him help me do things before the baby came. I would let him rub my stomach and go to my appointments. I would tell Monte that he would have a big role in his little sister's life. When she was born, I would let him hold her often and even hold her bottle with me while I feed her. Monte was so helpful at his age. I was a parent that introduced my children to God. I was one that trained them in the way they should go. I was brought up that away myself so I know we could stray away because I did myself at a time in my life. I also know prayer changes things because I'm a living witness. It's so much I could write about him. I didn't want to leave out anything but I'm sure it all cannot go in a book.

□

As time go on with my life with Monte not in my presence, God gives me moments and memories I thought I forgot. I can recall a time in his innocence that I had girlfriends of mine that would come over. We would eat the food I prepared, laughed a lot and just enjoyed each other's friendship. A friend of mine would play around with Monte, telling him how handsome he was and that he was her little boyfriend. His shy self would just listen. Until one day, she was leaving and saying good-bye to him and he broke out in tears. It just hurt his little heart and we all were amazed by his reaction. He was so quiet and emotionless at times but when he wanted to show his love for others, he did whether it was a hug, him quietly sitting next to you or his yes ma'am and no sir responses. We would go to church and he was even quiet there. He was in the choir, ushered and served when needed. He always was willing to help. He was his father's first and only child. His father's family was so excited about him because they believed he would never have or could have a child. He was already special in their hearts. On my side of the family, he was special too because we simply do that with all of our family. He wasn't the oldest but the first boy in my immediate family. My brothers treated him like their son. They inquired about him and tried to help him make the right decisions especially as he got older. One of my brothers was delivered from the street. Monte also was also a leap year baby. We were able to celebrate his birthday on Thanksgiving Day when it would fall on it.

Tests, Trials and Tribulations

Thank you God that he is reaching ages that children around him were not. May his cousin's soul rest in the arms of our loving God. His cousin, who he cared for, life was taking away. I don't know the whole story nor will I guess what happened but I know it affected Monte. However, it didn't stop him from continuing in the life I didn't want for him. The phone rings and I hear, "Hello is this Monte mother?" "Yes!" "Monte told me to call you because they locked him up. Monte was locked up for selling drugs. They didn't see the transaction but he did have drugs on him." The young man also let me know that Monte would be out on his own recon since this was his first offence. My heart drops because what I never wanted to happen happens. What I tried my best to protect him from and talk him away from has now happened. As his mother and once my heart calmed down, I began to pray for him. He comes home with us but there are still rules you have to follow. This is how we were brought up. Yes, there is a curfew. Yes, you do have to enroll in school somewhere even if it was to obtain his GED. Yes, we go to church, so you have to as well while living under this roof.

He went against all of this because hanging in the streets is better right now in his eyes. I can recall him calling me to tell me often he was locked up. Since these offences were minor, he was able to come home a lot. There were times that Monte didn't come in at a decent time and I couldn't sleep. I would be tossing and turning. I would ask my husband to ride me around at 3 am looking for him. Several officers would tell him to get out of the area. They were looking out for him because they saw him grow up in the area and knew his father. I remember when one officer let me know he always would say something to Monte about what he should be doing. Then there was a time when his choices caught up with him and he had to do time. He would write and say how sorry he was for getting in trouble and that he loved us. We would go visit him and I didn't ever want to do that especially when I use to do it with his father. I can recall hating to go visit his father when Monte was born. He was incarcerated and I told him I wasn't bringing my son to that place. He didn't see Monte until he came home six months after he was born. Yes, it hurts my heart to see my son behind bars and that he tried to keep us separate from the lifestyle he lived. People would say is that your mother and his response to them was to mind their business or I would ask him questions about what he was doing and he would say, "Ma, it's okay don't worry." I couldn't recall all of the reasons why he was locked up but I remember possession of drugs, distribution of drugs and loitering a lot. I would tell him the stuff my grandmother used to tell me when I was hanging out doing my own stuff and not in a relationship with God any longer. She would say, "You know God loves you and this not the life He has for you. God loves you no matter what and I can return to Him. You know you need to get your life straight." These are all the things I would say to him reminding him that I love him and praying for him. When he had court dates, he would always call me and say, 'Ma, pray." I would always tell him you caused this trouble and of course he would get mad but the truth is the truth. He would say, "Okay Ma, okay. Could you just pray?" When God answered and wouldn't give him what he deserved, I would remind him of God while he would try to tell me what his dad told him what to do from his experience in the system like he knew it all. I know it was nobody but God. Monte had a lot of trials that he should have spent time in jail longer than what was given according to the law but yet God had many of them dismissed.

Psalm 103:10 NIV

"he does not treat us as our sins deserve or repay us according to our iniquities."

We were connected with Greater Grace, which had a separate schooling for children like Monte trying to stay a step ahead as he was becoming older. They said he might not be able to go back in the public-school system. He did so well. His grades increased and he loved going to that school. I really loved it because my prayers were answered. The school was a Christian based school with biblical principles. They did a devotional in the morning. He had workbooks to bring home. It was all about the student one on one even though it was a small class. He did three years there before the school was shut down and he had to go back into the Baltimore City Public Schools because I couldn't afford to send him to Greater Grace's other school. My hope was interrupted for a moment and so was his.

Monte is now entering into the 10th grade at Lake Clifton High School and he decided that he couldn't deal with it or wouldn't deal with it. The streets offered him more. He decided to drop out of school. The spiral effect begins. We had family members that would try to help and get him jobs so he could stay off the streets until we got him ready for his GED. I remember a time when he worked at the movie theater doing janitorial. Monte would still get in trouble because he worked at night but he had idle time during the day. The new rules were to stay home during the day while I was at work. He thought he could hang out and beat me home not realizing I had people that would inquire about him when they saw him roaming about. The contract ended on the movie theater job, so he was hired at a restaurant as a dishwasher, which he did not like. I am sure he didn't like it because of the hours, washing dishes and not enough money. Money on the streets looked good to him and he decided to quit the job. I am sure many are wondering where his biological father was during these times. He would communicate with his dad and his dad would do for him but couldn't be the father he needed to be because of his own upbringing. He needed a father that would teach him the importance of education and to stay off the corners. His father was a product of what I didn't want for him. His father didn't have his father in his life. Yes, we can say well that's all the reason for him to be a father but he did try. Many have to deal with their own lives before they can pour into another, which is something his dad didn't do. I can remember a time when his father did step in to tell him, that street life wasn't good from his own experience. My heart dropped for his father at Monte's response. He told his father, "Man you can't tell me nothing." In all truth, he couldn't when that's all my son saw and how involved his dad was in that life, which led to his constant incarceration. The summer was upon us and I couldn't have him constantly out on the streets. We decided to punish him for an entire summer. He had to do school work, stay in his room and only go out with me. It hurt me for a moment but I would try anything to get him straight. He went through it, upset and all. It put some tension in our relationship. In the midst of trying to find a school that will accept him, he is now 17 and public school will not accept you but will send you to GED programs. I sent him out to classes but to my surprise or not, he was not attending. Lord, what I do now, he is not going to the program, he comes in late and hangs where I didn't want him to? Where did I go wrong was the question in my mind? I can't think about this right now. I can't do this right now. I have a daughter to think about as well.

He moves in or let me say, stays with his dad. I am sure where he can do what he wants. Would I say a little peace for me at the moment? No. I worried even more. At least when he was home, I can see how he was doing. I would call and check on him but I am sure I was lied to many times. I would constantly pray that God would keep him. God allowed him out once again and he began to live on his own but still doing his thing. I would watch the news and my heart would drop of the breaking news of someone who had been shot. I would say a prayer at that moment. Lord please don't let that be my child. At this moment as I write, I have noticed from all the memories and moments shared with Monte that prayer really does change things. I thank God because even though I wanted better for him. I thank God that he heard my prayers and answered all of them at the time. He covered, protected and didn't give Monte what he rightly deserved. God was merciful towards Monte each day of his life. God was faithful to Monte's mother all the way to the end. I would like to now take the time to pray for every mother and person that purchased this book.

I pray that you have a prayer life for your children and yourself. I pray that no matter what it looks like that you don't lose hope in the God of our lives in Jesus Name. I pray that your love covers the multitude of sins that your son, daughter, family or friends carry the same way our God covered ours and still does in Jesus name. I pray in the name of Jesus that you accept all that God says to you concerning your loved one that it takes over every negative thought and that you see beyond what you see for its by Faith that we believe and not sight in Jesus Name. I pray that God will heal your broken heart as

you cast all your care upon him for he cares for you and we know that God is nearer to the broken hearted in Jesus Name, I pray that your life began to touch someone else that have been waiting for you to be free that they may be free for whom the Son set free is free indeed. In Jesus Name. I pray in the name of Jesus that all curses will be broken starting with you and trickle down to your loved ones as the anointing of God destroys all yokes in Jesus Name. God, we give you glory, honor and praise for all that you are doing in our sight and behind the scenes, we thank you for peaceful and restful nights in you as you care for us and our family. We thank you for allowing your word concerning us and our loved ones to go out and not come back void unto you but to go out and establish that thing you called it to do and it prosper in Jesus name, amen.

When we moved to another house and Monte was back and forth to jail, it was in my mind that he couldn't come with us living that life. I didn't want drugs in my house even though I knew he would probably tell me it wasn't there. We had moved across the street from my mom and uncle. In my mind, this should work because there are more people to keep an eye on him, while I was working or just because it was needed. When we were trying to steer him in the right direction, I could remember coming home and talking to my fiancée, who is now my husband, as I was cleaning my daughter's bed. Underneath her pillow was drugs. Right away, I knew it was Monte with no thought of possibly being my daughter's. Heated as I was, I threw them in the toilet and flushed every pill. I was heartbroken, mad and angry because every talk, every visit to jail and every family member or friend he would see or know that died from this lifestyle did nothing to make him want to stop. Once he entered my home, I began to give him that same talk as usual. You need to stop! You're going to get killed out there! It's better things in life than this, etc. Then an add on came that I never thought I would do and I let my child know that I will not have this in my house. I wouldn't jeopardize his sister's life at all. It now became more

about his sister since he was showing me he didn't care about his actions. He gave me that same feeling that I had concerning his father and uncle when I confronted them. They just didn't care about others at that moment nor themselves to live that life. They knew it affected those around them even if they didn't believe it.

As bad as it hurt me, I had to put him out of my house. I had already made that decision before I talked to him. I prayed to God that my son would not hold any grudges against me nor think that I didn't love him. It was because I love him that I had to do it. It's called that tough love. You make people make decisions whether they make the right one or not. You also let them know when it comes to you boundaries are set. You control what people will put you in and what you're not going to accept.

I was not writing for a couple of days because I had to attend to a friend. She was going through her journey and I saw her laying on the church pews because she wasn't feeling well. I began to talk to God concerning her. God we can all encourage her, say what we think is the right thing but nobody is in her body nor do we know all the pain she is feeling. God reminded me of my grandson who was born

21bs. 2ounces and how the hospital where he was born would send Nuns and Chaplains to hold him, pray for him and comfort him while we were home until we saw him again. I remember going there one day to visit him and they placed a blanket over him. It was ski blue and white and had a prayer note attached to it with a name and number. My heart felt so good to know that he was being covered not only by the blanket but the prayers of others. That made me think of getting one for my friend because they did adults as well. I got in contact with Pastoral Care and they were more than happy to assist me. I wanted to give back for what they did for my grandson so I became a Volunteer Pastor Care person for two years. The next day after I contacted the office. We met up so I could get the blanket for my friend. The reverend and I were so happy to see each other because we haven't seen each other since 2012 and now it's five years later and my life has changed for the both of us. We shared, cried and laughed. This is the moment that God brought back to my attention why I needed to insert this here in this book. She has a son close to the age of my son who died. He is with someone that doesn't go to church and her son has not gone either. As a mother you want your children to do what you have taught them. You want it to continue as they are on their own. Sounds familiar doesn't it? I am aware and sure many of you felt that way or still do. It's a Mother's Love. We have a connection with our children. She proceeded to talk about her concerns with him and while she was talking, God started talking to me and my eyes began to swell up in tears. She inquired about what God was saying. She knew something was taking place. God told me to tell her that her son was at church and that he was talking to the young lady. This is the route they had to take. They will be in a building. Yes, it is important to assembly ourselves together in a building because God said so but we are not limited to a building because God is bigger than that. God said for us to train a child in the way he should go and when he is old, he will not depart from it. (Proverbs 22:6) Even though our children may stray away or not live the way you have taught them, you must believe that the Holy Spirit will bring all things back to their remembrance. God really does have them. Keep praying and holding on to God's promise concerning your children. His promises are Yes and Amen. It has to come to pass. God's word doesn't go or come back void unto Him but will accomplish what God desires and achieve the purpose for which he sent it. (Isaiah

55:11)

I am going all the way with God as I continue to write this book. As a parent, we often want to think of the good things rather than the bad things. Always remember that all things work for the good to those that love God and are called according to his purpose, even your children are included in that. (Romans 8:28) I was talking to a cousin of mine who is already seven years younger than Monte. We were at our grandmother's 93rd birthday celebration. He let me know he came across a picture of Monte and himself. He stated that he had a moment and then said, "Aunt Linda, which they called me even though I was their cousin lol. Monte was good especially to me." My heart just melted because despite what the world may say, some of them anyway. Monte through the eyes of others and God was what mattered. God sees the heart of man and not the outer appearance. God knows what is in all of our hearts even when our actions can speak otherwise. "For I know the thoughts that I think toward you, saith the Lord, thoughts of peace, and not of evil, to give you an expected end." (Jeremiah 29:11) You may see a lot of the same scriptures and it's okay. These scriptures I used when it came to Monte and I still use them today. I had to visit my little cousin's home that

Monday after the celebration. We laughed and conversed about Monte. He let me see the pictures he had. I noticed it was a school picture. He had to have been at least 12 or 13 and the way he posed for it made my heart happy. A smile came upon my face because I saw my innocent child. It made me feel good to see that even though I'm sure at the time that picture was taking, things started to change with him and his behavior. He still had something good in him. That is how God sees all of us. There is still some good in us. My cousin and I began to talk about the good ole days when he would come over and stay with Monte and how they would have so much fun as little boys. He also let me know that Monte always looked out for him. He could recall a time when he was at his aunt's house who lived around the corner from me. When he became bored, he would cut through the playground down the street from me just to hang with Monte. We talked about how I would fix meals for them and they would always have snacks in between. He even mentioned that as he came running through the playground to get to my house, that Monte saw him afar off and would warn him. He said if that is Beady, run back because he knew something was getting ready to happen. He trusted Monte so much that he always listened to him and just ran back in the opposite direction.

I want to encourage those who have boys that are testing you right now. Hold on to the promises of God covering your child. Look to God in everything concerning them. Pour into them as much good as you can. Know that God really does see all, knows all and is in control of it all. 2 Corinthians 5:7 states, "We walk by Faith and not sight." Don't let what you presently see dictate the outcome of your child but let your prayers and the word of God do that. As you read on in the latter part of this book, you will see that God has truly not only answered my prayers but the latter part of Monte's life as well.

A Promise

Kept

When my grandson had hearing problems, I spoke to his ear and said to his ear to hear from its original state. My daughter had high blood pressure, which she never had before. It was causing my grandson's heart rate to rise while he was in her womb. I would speak to her pressure and tell it to calm down and I would speak to his heart rate and tell it to beat at its original state that God created it. My son was dealing with his kidneys shutting down and his urine was literally black. His muscles in his body were collapsing and they had to give him shots in his belly. The doctor had to inform him that if he didn't come in the time he did, he would have died literally. I began to pray to his kidneys and muscles. I began to tell them to operate in their original state. Monte was hospitalized for at least two weeks and they were talking about putting him on dialysis. I had to pray day and night until what I prayed for became manifested. His urine came back to its original color. He left there without being on dialysis with instructions to drink plenty of water, cranberry juice and take his medication. He became hospitalized because he was ripping and running the streets, not drinking water and drinking alcohol. God kept him and gave us three more years with him before he died. He moved in with his sister after his last incarceration. He came home six months after his daughter was born. Living with his sister was a blessing for him as well as us. His sister reminded him to take his meds, got his prescriptions filled and cooked for him. She made sure he ate since he would be running around a lot. It helped me to know where he was and that he was being taken care of. He started to have a regular routine. One we could bank on. He would come in the house at night around 10 pm nightly and would leave the house no later than 12 pm the next day. He was still living that street life. One thing I can remember whether you agree with what I say or not, is that once I put him out he never included us in his outside life. He never wanted us to come around the area he was in and never wanted people to know who we were. I believe he was protecting us from that lifestyle. I am sure he shared a lot with his sister but never me. She used to tell me, "Ma, he's okay. He knows what he is doing. Don't worry." Then while at my grandmother's house to visit her I got the worst call of my life. My daughter on the other line is crying uncontrollably while she is at work because her girlfriend, who was at her house babysitting my grandson, believes my son is dead. After trying to calm my daughter, the young lady tells my daughter why she believes he is dead. Monte always leaves at 12 pm or sooner as I stated earlier. On this day, she checked on him at 10 am and he was still asleep. She continued with her morning but now it is 12 pm and he still sleeps, so she left him alone. She figured he had a long night because they knew he was high the night before and had been partying. Now it seemed too long to her because it was now 1 pm and he has not come out of his room. She goes and tries to awake him. She touches him and his body is cold and unmovable. The continued phone call from my daughter is, "Ma, Monte died." My heart dropped and my legs gave in. I collapsed on the floor and the voice I hear right away is what God promised me concerning my son years before. God said, "I told you I was going to change him in a moment in a twinkling of any eye." To hear my son is dead and God speak as well was so overwhelming. My daughter was at work so I wasn't near her either. I contacted my husband to tell him and for him to pick me up because I still needed to get to my son even though he was dead and get to my daughter.

As I arrived, my daughter was already there and I didn't want to see my son like that laying on his bed face down in his pillow. You would have thought he committed suicide the way his body was faced but he slept on his stomach anyway. While we were waiting for whomever to come when death takes place in homes, my four-year-old grandson was there and saw everything. He was the only one walking around like everything was okay. He was saying, "Uncle Monte gone grandma and that he was with

———————————————— •⟨⟩•⟨⟩• ————————————————

Jesus." It was like he knew what death was all about even though we haven't had this discussion with him. The coroner asked if we wanted to see him once they turned him over and we agreed. It was so hard that my daughter dropped to her knees. Who would have thought that he would die before me? His room was filled with alcohol bottles and many wanted to say he died from drugs and Percocet. My daughter was hurt that those rumors were going around. She took her anger out on many. I had to let her know what God said and that I believe he died of seizures, his epilepsy. I had to let her know you let people talk but believe God despite it all. It was time for her to see that God was in control of all of this because of the many prayers that went up on Monte's behalf. I had no insurance on him and now comes more tests but the promises of God out weigh it all. We had $2,500 but needed $3,500 more to have his funeral and bury him. I prayed to God continually and many helped. God showed us that despite how others feel what we should do. Friends and family helped out with getting what was needed. Should we have gone through this, now? No, but we had to and when it was all over, we were able to pay for his funeral and have money left over. The one thing that hurt me the most is that someone suggested we wait another week to bury him. How can someone say that to a person dealing with the death of their child? We proceeded on trusting God. My daughter was the biggest help ever. She held me at night when I had moments. She took care of all her brother's funeral arrangements. I was so grateful to her and even until this day, I haven't revisited his gravesite because of what I believe but she has been there to make sure things are well. I will eventually take care of things for his daughter's sake. The funeral has gone on and now it was time to hear about the cause of death. The coroner calls at least a couple of weeks later. "Mrs. Diggs, I am calling you to let you know the cause of your son's death." My heart drops again simply because I hear death and son again. She stated that he died from a seizure, epilepsy. I asked if she saw any drugs or alcohol in him. She says, "Mrs. Diggs, the only thing we saw in him was his medication." I paused and cried at the same time and said, thank you. I'm one who just believes God. One who holds on to His word until he brings it to pass, even if I have to remind myself when it doesn't look like it's going to happen. Even when others talk against what is going to happen. I couldn't wait to tell my daughter so she can see that God had it all along. The days of when it's all over. The phone calls stop and you left to wonder why and is this really real? Other mothers came to encourage me, especially, those whose sons died but our son didn't die the same way. They told me how I would act, what would take place with me but none of those things happened. It had me concerned about me and why these things were not happening. I can still hear from God so I went away and took a break from everybody. I asked God why I was not feeling what they had felt.

God simply said because I made you OK with it. He literally did. I began to compare my experience with theirs. The streets didn't take my son's life. The God I serve, love and loved me and my Son despite what he got into, covered him with His love just as much as I did. He brought His promise to me concerning Monte to pass. God answered my prayers to cover him and protect him. God answered my prayers to keep him from all hurt, harm and danger. Know this: keep praying for your loved one, keep giving them God's word and believe God is faithful to answer. Not in our time but He has an appointed time for everything. I'm a living witness. God kept His promise to me all the way until death. I decided to go away just to regroup, get answers to some questions and to really take on what has just happened to me and my family. It was hard at times because even though I believed God, I still couldn't believe it happened to us. God's promised word came to pass, He is still speaking to me and giving me peace through it all. Guess that's the flesh part of us that interferes with the Spirit side of us. That's why in a moment we can be okay with what takes place in life because of who we believe and worship. We worship God in spirit in truth. God is Spirit and those who worship him must worship in spirit and truth. Death was evident for Monte as well as us all and the promise was spoken, reminded and came to pass but I had to believe that among what I saw and even heard. We walk by Faith and not by sight.

Jeremiah 29:11 NIV

For I know the plans I have for you," declares the Lord, "plans to prosper you and not to harm you, plans to give you hope and a future.

Everlasting

Somethings will be everlasting. May 1st appears again in 2016 and it came upon me so fast. I had some errands to run and was with a childhood friend. We were about to have lunch together after a golf tournament I attend yearly. As I sat in the car to wait for her while listening to music and scrolling through Facebook, the Spirit reminded me that fast, in that moment that it was May 1st. I began to thank God because now I was in another place in accepting or let me say being okay with Monte not being here. It didn't affect me like it did the two previous years where I was always ready for this day. My mind would be all over the place and I would be crying uncontrollably. I didn't know if it was because in between the date approaching God would give me short moments throughout a day or just because and I am sure God strengthens me and comforts me for moments to come. I was so in awe that I called my daughter and asked her if she knew what day this was and her response, "Yes ma." I asked her if she was okay and she said, "Yes ma, I really am."

Sometimes in death of a loved one, you never know if you will be okay or how you will get through this even if you are able. It was not a getting through for me; it is a living with it. It's EVERLASTING. I would never tell anyone it is easy. I will never tell no anyone to get over it. I will tell someone, when you put your love one in the hands of God from the very beginning and let God know your true heart concerning them, that God will give you a word of hope. Something to hold onto and it will happen. Trust Him to keep you through it all for God is faithful to His word for He is the word. John 1:1 states, "In the beginning was the Word, and the Word was with God, and the Word was God." Read John 1 1:4 in its entirety! The Lord really helped me on that day and I was able again to live on. Moments still came after that date. Let me explain moments. Moment mean:

1. A very brief period

2. Importance, significance.

My moments are not too many past moments but right now and future moments of Monte. I can recall a moment while holding Amoni, Monte's daughter, he wouldn't get to see her grow up, finish school, get married or have her own family. Yes, this brought tears to my eyes. To really hit home with my moments. Monte died at the age of 27 years old. He didn't graduate from school. He didn't have a career. He wasn't married nor did he have his own home. Now I realize these are some of the things I will not see, nor get to share with him. When we have family gatherings, not only will he not be there but none of his future life will be either. We have our wonderful granddaughter but it's nothing like a mother seeing her child/children accomplish many things in life. Did I ever feel like I have been robbed of those things? I do but I am so grateful to God and His way of carrying me through this life of my moments. It is really preparing me ahead of time not to feel robbed, nor in regret, nor sad, nor disappointed, nor upset, nor bothered, nor being hateful towards God. Living in the NOR of life with God. Read Romans 8:39 in its entirety! What I am is in a place to want to help others with the death of their loved ones. I am concerned about others' trust and relationship with God because of the death of their loved ones. Also knowing that this will help a parent with a child/children that are alive and living to revert to the right way.

Acknowledgments

I truly have to thank God first because without Him this would not be possible. It was and is God's word that has been keeping me. Also I'm thankful for my husband, Antoine Diggs, who pushes me in whatever God has placed upon my heart and always remind me of who I am and the writing that was in me. I thank my Mom, Laverne Hill- Shaw, who always calls me special and even gave me the title of the books that will be published. I give thanks to all my family and friends, especially, Minister Best friend, Phyliss Harper, for keeping me accountable to get this book out. Last but not least, I'm thankful and grateful to you for purchasing this book and I believe God will comfort you through it.

Matthew 19:26b

With men this is impossible; but with God all things are possible.

Philippians 4:13

I can do all things through Christ who strengthens me.

About the Author

Linda Diggs is the founder and visionary of Still Life Community Outreach Inc. She has been endowed with a teaching, preaching gift to present the Gospel message with simplicity. Being blessed with the spirit of Dorcas (Acts 9:36), she is also a Kingdom Intercessor. She is not only an active Minister, Leader of the Missionary Board and Outreach of her church but she has always had a love for all of God's people. She is also a graduate of The North Carolina School of Theology, with her BS in Biblical Studies and Masters in Theology. She is a wife, mother of two (Monte proceeded her in death), and grandmother to four beautiful grandchildren.

□